Pinpointing Issues with AWS Certificate Manager

Table of Contents

Chapter 1. Introduction

In this Special Report, we delve deep into understanding the intricate technologies underpinning AWS Certificate Manager, and herein, we shine a light on some of its most confounding issues. Don't get the impression that this is an arcane or inaccessible topic. Think of it as a journey of discovery, a journey that has direct implications for how we secure our digital platforms and communications. While the subject may seem complex for those new to the area, we've made sure to lay it out in a manner that is easy to understand, relatable, and practical. We unpack the possible problems that could arise, presenting nuanced solutions drawn from industry best practices and expert insights. This report, we assure, is a worthwhile investment for anyone seeking to refine their AWS operational efficiency and cybersecurity. Dive in, find out more, and equip yourself with the knowledge you need to master the AWS Certificate Manager.

Chapter 2. Introduction to AWS Certificate Manager

In many modern applications, secure communications form a vitally imperative role. To resolve this, Amazon Web Services (AWS) has developed the AWS Certificate Manager (ACM). Spearheading the act of the secure transmission of data, ACM plays a critical role in the world of network and data security.

AWS Certificate Manager allows users to manage the life cycle of SSL/TLS certificates including creation, deployment, renewal, and expiry. By preventing the exploitation of vulnerable data, it forms an impervious barricade safeguarding your digital information. As we delve into our exploration of this subject matter, we seek to equip you with an understanding of the ACM, leading to an assessment of how we manage secure communications and the implications of this knowledge for contemporary digital platforms. Let's embark on this exciting journey.

2.1. What is AWS Certificate Manager?

AWS Certificate Manager is a service that allows a user to easily provision, manage, and deploy public and private SSL/TLS certificates for use with AWS services and your internal connected resources. These certificates are used to secure network communications and establish the identity of websites over the Internet, as well as resources on private networks.

Perhaps the most compelling reason to use ACM is the reality that, once you secure a certificate, ACM continues to manage the certificate's life cycle, implementing automatic certificate renewals, and maintaining the secure status of applications. This means you can create and manage certificates without the need for specialized expertise, allowing you to keep your focus on your core business tasks.

2.2. How Does ACM Work?

At the heart of ACM's operations is the concept of a certificate lifecycle - a complex, multifaceted process that ranges from the creation of a certificate to its renewal or eventual retirement. ACM essentially functions behind the scenes, executing tasks that many AWS users might only vaguely understand.

To start with, you request a certificate by proving that you own or control the domain names that you want to include in your certificate. You can ask for validation of one or more domain names and for ACM to issue your certificate. After validation, ACM will issue an SSL/TLS certificate that you can use with other AWS services.

From there, ACM takes over, managing renewals, monitoring for potential issues or vulnerabilities, and ensuring your certificates remain valid and secure. If ACM could not renew the certificate, it sends an email to inform the domain owner.

2.3. Types of Certificates

Broadly speaking, ACM handles two types of SSL/TLS certificates: public and private.

Public certificates identify web sites over the internet and are validated by a public certificate authority (CA). This validation process helps to assure your users that your site's identity has been confirmed by a trusted third-party validator. ACM provides these certificates for free.

Private certificates, on the other hand, identify resources over a private network. They utilize an online certificate status protocol (OCSP) to check the revocation status of certificates. With ACM Private CA, you can create and manage private certificate authority (CA) hierarchies, including root and subordinate CAs.

Each of these kinds of certificates has its use cases and is essential depending on the specifics of the infrastructure you're operating on.

2.4. Benefits of AWS Certificate Manager

Now that you understand the foundational aspects of ACM, it's important to emphasize the benefits it offers.

First and foremost, ACM handles the complexities of certificate provisioning, deployment, and management. It issues trusted public and private certificates, automatically renews them, and deploys them to AWS resources, all without any user intervention.

Secondly, ACM eradicates expiring certificates' issues. As it triggers automatic renewals and monitors the certificate lifecycle, there's no need to worry about a certificate unexpectedly expiring and breaking your applications.

Lastly, ACM comes at no additional cost for public SSL/TLS certificates – it's included as part of your regular AWS service charges.

However, the powerful functionalities and tangible benefits of AWS Certificate Manager do not make it immune to several common issues and challenges, which we will explore in the subsequent sections of this report.

In conclusion, the AWS Certificate Manager is a crucial technology underpinning secure digital communications. We've covered its operations, the different types of certificates it handles, and its key benefits, let's move forward to a detailed discussion on the operational and security challenges that could arise with its use, as well as the actionable insights on how to address these.

As we journey through the vast and fascinating landscape of ACM, we hope the complex becomes accessible, the daunting becomes manageable, and the unknown becomes familiar. Now, let's continue our exploration, and take another step forward towards mastering AWS Certificate Manager.

Chapter 3. Delineating the Problems: The Real Face of the Issues

It's critical to understand that any tech utility, irrespective of its visibility, is susceptible to issues. The same applies to AWS Certificate Manager (ACM), which is complex due to its significant interlinkages with other AWS services. This complexity could lead to problems that demand our attention.

3.1. Troubleshooting Common Issues

One of the most frequent issues with AWS ACM revolves around wildcard domain validation failures. Amazon ACM supports wildcard domains, which can be used to protect several subdomains with a single certificate. However, when you encounter domain validation errors, you might be led down a confusing path. Check for asterisk (*) placement in the domain name; an incorrect position often castrates the wildcard. A correctly set domain name should mimic *.example.com.

Another common problem is attempting to revalidate a domain with an expired or deleted certificate. The ACM service offers suggestions to rectify this issue:

- Verify that the ACM certificate status is 'Issued.'

- Confirm that the domain's DNS validation record has been added to the DNS provider's configuration.

- Ensure that Route 53 alias records are correctly configured for both the domain and any subdomains.

However, it's crucial to understand that these are not one-size-fits-all solutions. The nature of your IT infrastructure and operations will often necessitate a more custom approach.

3.2. Unexpected Limitations

AWS ACM holds strict limitations that can sometimes elicit the "Too many certificates already issued for the exact set of domains" error. This predicament appears due to the ACM's current request limit that allows merely 2000 active certificates per account per region.

One possible solution here is to consolidate your domains by using a wildcard certificate that would cover multiple domain names, which significantly increases your operational efficiency.

3.3. Delicate Dependencies and Integration Issues

While ACM's tight-knit integration with other AWS services is among its biggest strengths, it can also be a weakness. For instance, CloudFront only accepts SSL certificates from ACM, and Load Balancers often generate problems in relation to multiple subdomain SSL certificates.

Dependencies between ACM and services like Elastic Load Balancer (ELB), AWS Elastic Beanstalk, and Amazon CloudFront must be carefully managed using Amazon Route 53. Any misalignment could impede service performance, making it crucial for teams to ensure they have a firm grasp of how these services interoperate.

3.4. Misunderstood Expiration Dates

ACM Certificates are set to expire 13 months after they have been issued. When certificate renewal isn't handled correctly, users can encounter problems. The automatic renewal should usually avert this crisis, but manual intervention might be necessary when DNS validation records don't exist or have been altered.

Also, users need to be aware of the ACM's renewal checks which start 45 days before the certificate expiration date. Keeping tabs on this timeframe can help them avoid service disruptions or outages.

3.5. Lost ACM Private Keys

While the ACM-managed renewal process prevents most mishaps, losing ACM private keys can still pose a problem. This is because for ACM-managed certificates, AWS maintains the private keys securely but also transparently, meaning you cannot download it.

Should you require the private key for any form of server-side TLS, you might be better off opting for a self-managed certificate. Take heed, though, as with the self-managed route, you handle the key security and certificate rotation.

To summarize, while ACM does indeed have its share of problems, familiarizing yourself with its common issues can make for smoother sailings. The real face of the issues lies not in the problems themselves but our understanding and response to them. When embarking on your digital transformation journey with AWS, it's wise to arrive prepared and aware. Notably, maintaining a human-operable monitoring system for your ACM can prevent many issues from escalating in the first place. So, dive in, keep learning, and let your digital passages be guided by robust and secure practices.

Chapter 4. Decoding the Issue of Certificate Expiration

Before we can fully grasp the issue of certificate expiration, let's take a moment to understand what certificates are within the context of AWS Certificate Manager (ACM). In essence, ACM is a service that maintains and deploys SSL/TLS certificates needed to enable secure network connections. SSL and TLS are cryptographic protocols used to secure data communication over an untrustworthy network, such as the internet.

Certificates follow what's called the Public Key Infrastructure (PKI); they bind a public key with respective user identities, ensuring the integrity and authenticity of communication. Because certificates ensure secure data transmission, keeping them up-to-date and valid is crucial, and herein lies our major topic of discussion - the complex issue of certificate expiration.

4.1. Understanding the Importance of Certificate Life Cycle

The life cycle of a certificate is dictated by its validity period. When issued, a certificate is given an expiration date, typically between one to two years. Let's break it down:

1. Certificate Request: The life cycle begins when an entity submits a certificate signing request (CSR) to the Certificate Authority (CA), containing the public key and the subject (like the entity's name). The requester retains the private key securely.

2. Issuing: The CA then validates the CSR's data, issues the digital certificate, and publicly posts it to its repository.

3. Expiration: When the certificate's validity period ends, it expires.

It's no longer trusted for use in secure communication.

Certificate expiration plays a crucial role in maintaining a robust security posture - it limits the timeframe attackers have to crack the private key associated with a certificate. The shorter the validity period, the less time a potential malicious actor has to exploit the certificate if compromised.

4.2. Certificate Expiration and its Implications

Now that we have a basic understanding of certificate expiration, the next step is to delve into the problems it presents.

Problem 1: Service Disruptions - An expired certificate effectively brings your service to a standstill. When a user's browser finds an expired certificate, it blocks the user from accessing the server to protect user data. Navigational warnings and error displays deter users, interrupting business functioning and IT operations.

Problem 2: Security Threats - While the idea of certificate expiration was devised as a security measure, it paradoxically also presents a potential security threat. If these expired certificates are not replaced in time, your services become vulnerable to attacks, such as man-in-the-middle (MITM) attacks.

Problem 3: Brand Erosion and Loss of Trust - Brand and trust erosion is an indirect yet significant impact of certificate expiration. Users swiftly lose trust in your services when they encounter warning messages or navigation blocking due to certificate expiration. This customer dissatisfaction can lead to loss of business and harm a company's reputation.

4.3. Tackling Certificate Expiration

Handling certificate life cycle management in a large-scale environment can be challenging, prone to human error, and time-consuming. Here are some solutions that take the pressure off and help streamline the process:

Solution 1: Automatic Certificate Renewal – AWS Certificate Manager provides automatic certificate renewal for Amazon-issued certificates so that you don't have to do manual work. ACM handles the renewal and deployment of these certificates, ensuring uninterrupted secure communication.

Solution 2: Certificate Expiry Monitoring - You can configure Amazon CloudWatch Events to get notified before the expiration dates of certificates. These preemptive alerts allow teams to act in time, renewing certificates before they cause service disruptions.

Solution 3: Implementing Shorter Certificate Life Spans - Although this means you will replace certificates more frequently, shorter life spans can decrease the potential window of vulnerability if a private key is compromised.

4.4. Best Practices for Certificate Expiration

While automation and monitoring provide a much-needed helping hand, remembering and implementing some best practices can further alleviate the risks of certificate expiration:

1. Always have a backup plan.

2. Plan certificate renewals well in advance.

3. Avoid using long-lived certificates.

4. Set up a robust monitoring and alert system.

5. Test the end-to-end certificate renewal process periodically.

Facing the challenge of certificate expiration head-on requires a sound understanding of the processes involved and a commitment to best practices. Technological intervention can alleviate some of the burden, but a commitment to maintaining tight control over certificate life cycle is paramount to successful navigation of this complex issue.

Chapter 5. Unraveling the Trouble with Cross-Account Certificates

Cross-account certification management is one of the features of AWS Certificate Manager (ACM) that allows organizations with multiple accounts to manage certificates centrally. While this feature adds a layer of efficiency and governance, it also holds its share of perplexing issues as it navigates through the twists and turns of AWS' multi-account structure.

5.1. Understanding Cross-Account Certificates

Cross-account certificates, when used prudently, can be a powerful instrument to generate seamless certificate operations across multiple accounts. An AWS account that creates or owns a certificate is referred to as the certificate owner. This primary account can then share the certificate with other AWS accounts, known as members, while wielding extensive control over permissions and rules.

However, cross-account certificates pose a series of challenges when it comes to sharing certificates, propagating changes, maintaining access levels, dealing with Advanced Resource Access Management (RAM) rules, understanding IAM policies, and much more. These challenges have significant implications on error management, security aspects, and the overarching governance across multiple accounts.

5.2. Overcoming the Difficulty of Sharing Certificates

Sharing a certificate across different AWS accounts, while fundamentally an uncomplicated process, involves a few steps that can quickly become overwhelming. There is a need to understand the implications of shared ownership, the rules surrounding it, and foresee the potential issues that can arise during and after the sharing process.

The best practice is to create a well-articulated process whereby the sequence of the steps is followed meticulously. This approach can include actions such as making the certificate shareable, defining permissions, sharing the certificate, and confirming that its status is 'active' in the member account. Issuing thorough guides that cover every detail of these steps will significantly reduce mistakes and mismanagement.

5.3. Navigating Propagation of Changes

Another challenge with cross-account certificates is the propagation of changes. Some alterations made by the certificate owner, such as renewing a certificate or updating its configuration, do not automatically replicate across the member accounts.

To handle this, automation can play a critical role. Scripting the renewal or configuration update process can yield substantial results. Furthermore, creating alerts and notifications for upcoming renewals or necessary updates could help administrators keep a tight grip on the certificates' lifecycle.

5.4. Managing Access Levels

Access level management is crucial in cross-account operations. Differentiating between the certificate owner and members poses challenges, especially when trying to avoid giving members excessive permissions. This can lead to the risk of compromising the security of certificates.

IAM policies can be leveraged to govern access to the certificates. The right mix of permissions needs to be granted to members. By using least privilege policies and the permission boundaries feature, all actions are under the control of the account owner while still providing necessary access to the members.

5.5. Resolving Advanced Resource Access Management Issues

Advanced Resource Access Management (RAM) rules are an essential part of cross-account certificates but can become a source of complexity due to the multifaceted guidelines that need to be followed.

To alleviate these concerns, detailed work instructions should be used. Proper guidance can help users understand the intricate aspects of RAM rules and their implications on the usage of certificates. A thorough knowledge transfer, meticulous documentation, and a reliable support system can help resolve issues associated with RAM rules.

5.6. Addressing Intricacies of IAM Policies

IAM policies are a fundamental part of the AWS Certificate Manager.

However, the sheer complexity and the intricate layers of these policies can make it challenging for users to adopt. The problem exacerbates when these policies interact with ACM, leading to a variety of issues.

The answer lies in simplifying the language and the structure of these policies to make them more understandable, and developing a standard set of policies to help eliminate the burden of custom policy creation for every user. It is also crucial to regularly update the knowledge base and provide training on the changes to ensure that everyone can understand and use these policies effectively.

5.7. Conclusion

Although the AWS Certificate Manager's cross-account certificates present numerous complications, these challenges are surmountable with adequate understanding, management, automation, and policy mastery. However, the journey toward mastering these certificates requires consistent learning, meticulous planning, and an approach rooted in best practices of cybersecurity. With the right guidance and concerted effort, it's possible to unravel the complex world of AWS cross-account certificates, paving the way for a seamless and secure business operation.

Chapter 6. The Search for High Availability: DNS Challenges

AWS Certificate Manager facilitates the process of managing the lifecycle of SSL/TLS certificates, which are relied on to provide secure, encrypted communications between clients and servers. However, this process is fraught with challenges related to high availability, particularly when it comes to matters of Domain Name System (DNS) implementations.

6.1. Understanding High Availability

High Availability (HA) refers to a system or component that is continuously operational for a significantly long length of time. For websites and web services, it's pivotal to ensure maximum uptime and minimal downtime. A key challenge faced in the pursuit of High Availability is obtaining a reliable DNS service.

The DNS is the phonebook of the internet, translating human-friendly website names to IP addresses that machines can understand. Reminiscent of indexing in a book, DNS allows fast access to content without needing to remember exact addresses. This translation process facilitates users accessing your content by using domain names like `www.example.com`.

However, if the DNS of the site fails, the site becomes inaccessible, leading to dreaded downtime. Managing DNS for high availability is a critical requirement for all web-based services but it's not without its complexities, especially when integrated with AWS Certificate Manager.

6.2. DNS and the Certificate Lifecycle

It starts with understanding that the life cycle of a certificate involves multiple stages: requesting, validating, issuing, and renewing. In the validation stage, AWS's Certificate Manager sends a DNS CNAME (Canonical Name) code to be added to your DNS entry for the domain associated with the certificate request. As it waits for a DNS change to propagate across the internet, several timing-related challenges can emerge.

Depending on DNS provider conditions, propagation of changes may take hours or even days. Consequently, this lends a dynamic and unpredictable element to certificate validation, folding uncertainty into the availability equation. It becomes pivotal to ensure DNS operations are scheduled and executed in a manner that smoothens this potentially disruptive process.

6.3. DNS Challenges and Strategies to Address Them

Among the common challenges with DNS in relation to high availability are DNS caching, Time to Live (TTL) considerations, redundant DNS services, record propagation delays, and the management of multiple DNS zones.

Maximizing DNS Cache Use: DNS caching, while designed to improve DNS query performance by storing DNS query results for a specific TTL, can become an issue if your DNS records change. As such, if you operate in an environment with frequent changes, ensure reduced TTL to minimize potential disruptions caused by stale records.

TTL Considerations: Deciding TTL flush periods ties into efficiently managing traffic loads on your servers. However, understanding the trade-off between request resolution times and DNS server loads is crucial in determining the optimal TTL setting.

Managing Redundant DNS Services: Offering a back-up or secondary DNS can prevent your site from going down if your primary DNS fails. However, synchronizing all changes made in the primary DNS to the secondary DNS presents a hurdle.

Understanding Propagation Delays: Delays in DNS record propagation can lead to service downtime if, for example, there are changes in web server IP addresses. This challenge can be mitigated by coordinating the IP address changes with DNS configuration updates.

Managing Multiple DNS Zones: AWS Route 53 provides DNS services for your Hosted Zones. However, dealing with numerous zones and ensuring they are correctly linked to the right resources can present a challenge. A good DNS manager that offers visibility and control can simplify the management of these zones.

These strategies offer a foundation upon which to construct your DNS for high availability. Keep in mind that the path to optimum DNS operation is enhanced by ongoing vigilance and proactive adjustments in response to constantly evolving operational situations.

6.4. Bringing it all Together

In summary, the AWS Certificate Manager can enhance your operation's cybersecurity significantly, but not without challenges regarding High Availability and DNS. Controlling caching, managing TTL, establishing redundant DNS services, planning for propagation delays, and correctly managing your Route 53 zones are all fundamental areas of focus.

Remember, an efficient and reliable DNS translates to improved high availability of your AWS services. Regardless of the complexities, harnessing AWS Certificate Manager effectively is a worthwhile endeavor, leading to improved security for your digital platforms and client communications. As such, understanding these issues regarding high availability is essential for anyone seeking to maximize their operational efficiency in the AWS environment.

Chapter 7. Dissecting the Setup Difficulties: Wrong Zone Troubles

Undoubtedly, one significant hurdle that many users experience while working with AWS Certificate Manager (ACM) is related to the wrong choice of zone during the setup process. Given the nature of AWS deployments, zone selection determines the availability and redundancy of your resources, and for the ACM, it directly impacts the applicability and functionality of the SSL/TLS certificates. So let's examine the what, why, and how of the erroneously chosen zone issues in detail.

7.1. Understanding AWS Zones

To comprehend the issue, it's important first to understand the role and significance of zones within the AWS ecosystem. Amazon Web Services (AWS) divides its infrastructure worldwide into Regions and Availability Zones (AZs). A Region is a geographical area, each consists of two (or more) Availability Zones. An AZ is essentially a data center. AWS operates multiple AZs within most of its regions for redundancy, ensuring that if one data center experiences an issue, AWS resources remain accessible.

ACM certificates, while they can be used globally, are managed within specific AWS regions. This means that for successful setup and the functioning of your ACM, the zone selection is critical.

7.2. The Wrong Zone Dilemma

Now, let's delve into the troubles that arise owing to incorrect zone set up.

1. Certificate Unavailability: If you create an ACM certificate in one region, it can't be used directly in other AWS services that are based in a different region. Thus, a common error when setting up AWS Certificate Manager involves selecting the wrong zone, rendering the certificate unavailable in the targeted zone where you want to use it.

2. Increased Latency: Incorrect zone selection can also increase latency. If your application server and your client are not in the same zone, it can extend the certificate verification time while establishing a secure TLS/SSL communications channel.

7.3. Mitigating the Wrong Zone Issue

Solving the wrong zone problem, in essence, consists of two parts: prevention and resolution. Let's explore both:

1. Initial Zone Setup and Precautions Prevention, indeed, is the best cure. Be cautious while you're initially setting up the ACM. Some considerations include:

   ◦ Always be aware of where your services are located. Each service in your AWS account gets a dedicated region. Make sure to select the region where you want to deploy the ACM certificate.

   ◦ For low latency and high speed, choose the zone closest to your end users.

   ◦ Understanding your specific requirements can lead you on the right path. For instance, some AWS services only work in certain regions.

2. Resolving After Misconfiguration Undoing a misconfigured zone can be challenging, but it's not impossible. Here's a step-by-step approach:

   ◦ First, identify the services that are using the wrongly deployed certificate. Track the dependencies. Do remember:

replacing a certificate may impact services that depend on it.

- Request a new ACM certificate for the right zone following the standard procedure.

- Update all the services and applications to use the newly issued certificate from the correct zone.

7.4. Conclusion

Though configuring the AWS Certificate Manager may seem daunting, with a clear understanding of the AWS infrastructure, particularly the role and selection of zones, it is manageable. Often, issues like wrong zone troubles arise due to a misunderstanding of essential concepts or missteps during setup. But with keen attention, accurate selection during configuration, and strategic problem-solving when issues arise, you can optimize your ACM experience, thereby enhancing the security and efficiency of your AWS deployment.

Chapter 8. Decoding Permission and Policy Issues

As navigators on our journey to demystify AWS certificate management, the labyrinth of permissions and policies forms a critical stopover. Herein we disentangle the complex machinery of permissions, comprehend its implications on AWS Certificate Manager (ACM), recognize policy concerns, and elucidate how to resolve the potential predicaments.

8.1. Understanding Permissions in ACM

Permissions in AWS are the cornerstone of secure access management. They determine the access levels of an IAM entity (user or role) to AWS services and resources.

To ensure secure access, AWS operates on the principle of least privilege - a user or a role has only the bare minimum permissions required to fulfill their function. For AWS certificate management, permissions automatically get attached to an ACM certificate when it is imported.

Now, you might wonder: What exactly are these permissions, and how are they associated? These permissions are included in the ACM certificate AWS provided policy named "AWS managed policy for certificate manager".

The permissions cover actions such as ListCertificates, DescribeCertificate, GetCertificate, etc. Broadly, these permissions allow users or roles to perform actions like viewing and listing all certificates, describing all details of a certificate or fetching a certificate. The 'Resource' field is defined as '*' meaning 'all resources' which allows unrestricted access to perform these actions on all certificates.

In addition to this, other permissions like 'ImportCertificate' and 'RequestCertificate' can be attached to the entities for allowing actions like importing and requesting certificates.

8.2. Permission-Related Concerns

While permissions come with the advantages of secure and controlled access, they can also pose issues if not appropriately handled, or in the event of misconfigurations.

1. *Unrestricted Access*: Under certain circumstances, you might find a wildcard '*' set for all actions in an IAM policy. This configuration implies unrestricted or full permissions. Unless extremely necessary, this is not a recommended configuration.

2. *Unintentional Denial of Access*: At times, unintentional errors such as misspecified resources or incorrectly formed actions may result in denial of access for legitimate users.

3. *Conflicting Policies*: AWS evaluates all policies associated with a user or role to determine the effective permissions. During this evaluation process, an explicit deny in any of these policies overrides all allow statements, leading to potential access issues.

8.3. Remedying Permission Issues

Knowledge of potential pitfalls is the first step towards solutions. Let's outline the remedial measures for each issue:

1. *Limiting Unrestricted Access*: If you find a wildcard '*' set for all actions in an IAM policy, it indicates too much 'permission' which is unhealthy. To remediate this, begin by reviewing the requirement for such settings. As AWS guidelines recommend,

aim to set the principle of least privilege.

For instance, if an entity only needs to request and list certificates, just attach 'ACM:ListCertificate' and 'ACM:RequestCertificate' permissions to the entity instead of giving full permissions.

1. *Mitigating Unintentional Access Denials*: To debug unintentional access denials, use IAM policy simulator or IAM access analyzer. These tools help you in analyzing the existing permissions set in IAM policies. After detecting the issue, refer to AWS policy grammar to write or modify your policies properly.

2. *Resolving Conflicting Policies*: Explicating conflicts amongst policies can be tricky. Start by reviewing all attached policies and look out for any explicit denies. If found, assess if such deny is necessary. Alternatively, you can consider restructuring your IAM entities and policies for cleaner management.

8.4. Understanding Policy Matters

Policies play a fundamental role in governing permissions within AWS. In AWS Certificate Manager, policies primarily operate at two levels - Identity Policies and Resource Policies. Identity Policies are attached to IAM entities (users, groups, and roles), whereas Resource Policies are attached to ACM resources (certificates).

Most of the policy-related concerns in ACM come from misconfigurations that stem from not understanding how these policies work. However, AWS has ample guides and examples to help understand how to use these policies proficiently.

8.5. Finding Remedies to Policy Problems

The first step in rectifying policy issues is identifying what aspect of the policy is causing the issue. This process involves understanding the role and flow of different elements in AWS policy grammar such as 'Effect', 'Action', 'Resource,' and 'Condition'.

An incorrect statement or misaligned condition can grant unwanted access or block necessary access. To solve such problems, start by trying to understand the error message, which often provides clues to the issue's source. Additionally, AWS provides the IAM policy validator tool that can be used to check your policies for syntax and grammatical mistakes.

Another common issue arises when resource policies are not in harmony with identity policies, causing access related issues. In such cases, AWS recommends re-evaluating your access strategy and adjusting your IAM and ACM policies accordingly.

In conclusion, understanding and managing permissions and policies is a central part of AWS certificate management. As with any journey, remember: it's not just about reaching your destination but about what you discover along the way. Whether it's managing permission-related issues or untangling policies, remember you're not alone - AWS has a plethora of manageable, pragmatic tools and resources to do the heavy lifting. With a profound appreciation and apt handling of permissions and policy matters, navigate confidently and make your journey through AWS Certificate Manager a seamless one.

Chapter 9. Unearthing the Complications with Renewal and Rotation

The quest to simplify and automate tasks is inherent in the nature of technology. Administrators leverage myriad services provided by AWS to achieve operational efficiency, and one such service is the AWS Certificate Manager (ACM). Undoubtedly, ACM has brought a significant shift in how we manage our SSL/TLS certificates, from orchestration to renewal. However, like any technology, it's not devoid of complexities. The management of certificate renewal and rotation is one such tangled area that often leaves the professionals scratching their heads.

9.1. Understanding Renewal and Rotation

Before diving into the technicalities, let's establish a common ground about what renewal and rotation of certificates mean. Certificate renewal refers to the process of applying for and receiving a new certificate after the existing one expires. On the other hand, rotation involves replacing the current certificate with a new one, irrespective of the remaining validity of the current certificate. The rotation can be for routine maintenance or due to a compromise in the certificate's integrity.

AWS Certificate Manager automates the renewal process for ACM-issued certificates and those imported that are still valid. This automation significantly alleviates the administrative burden. However, understanding how the automation works and dealing with instances where it fails are critical to maintaining the secure veneer of your AWS environment.

9.2. The Automation Behind Renewal

AWS manages the renewal process of the ACM Certificate, and this automation is enabled by default. ACM starts attempting to renew the certificate about 60 days before its expiration. AWS uses the previously validated domain information to validate the renewal request. Herein lies the first potential problem: suppose the initially validated information is no longer available or has changed. In that case, the automated renewal process is bound to fail.

In case of renewal failure due to validation, AWS tries every day until it successfully obtains the new certificate. However, if AWS can't renew the certificate within 22 days of expiration, it notifies the domain owner of the impending problem. Notably, ACM removes the expired certificate from your ACM account within 60 days after expiration. Hence, if you've used the expired certificate in another AWS service, ensure it's replaced before its removal to avoid potential service disruption.

9.3. Challenges in Automated Renewal

While AWS's Certificate Manager does an efficient job of certificate renewal, it's not without its challenges. Here are a few scenarios where the automated renewal process can cause inconvenience.

- If the email addresses used for domain validation aren't available anymore, automatic renewal will fail.

- Change in domain ownership can lead to renewal issues.

- In the case of DNS validation, if the DNS record has changed or is removed, ACM cannot verify the domain to renew the certificate.

- Certificates generated through methods like private CA do not auto-renew.

9.4. Rotation: Not as Simple as it Seems

While AWS automatically renews SSL/TLS certificates, it does not automatically rotate them, making the rotation process a bit complex. When a certificate needs to be replaced before it expires, AWS admins have to deal with the task manually. The rotation process varies based on whether you are rotating an Amazon issued certificate or an imported one.

To execute a rotation, admins must request a new certificate, add it to the ACM, and then update all AWS resources that use the old certificate to use the new one. Also, admins must consider factors like backward compatibility for older clients, potential service disruption, and the validity period of the new certificate.

9.5. Mitigating the Renewal and Rotation Complications

Given these complexities, it's crucial to build a safety net that can support your organization's cybersecurity goals whilst maintaining operational efficiency. Here are a few strategies:

- Regularly monitor certificate status by setting up Amazon CloudWatch alarms to receive notifications when a certificate is about to expire.

- Devise a Certificate Policy that includes regular audits to ensure that all resources are using a valid certificate.

- Opt for DNS validation, which remains valid as long as the ACM-issued certificate exists.

- Set up an automated process for certificate rotation. Use AWS Lambda for automation of certificate rotation tasks.

- Always replace expired certificates used in other AWS services before ACM removes them.

- Regularly update the email addresses used for validation.

===

In conclusion, even with the automation prowess of the AWS Certificate Manager, it's necessary to be proactive and thorough in your certificate renewal and rotation methodology. The road to mastering the AWS Certificate Manager is indeed rocky, but the journey would prove rewarding as it brings you one step closer to securing your digital platforms and achieving operational efficiency. Understanding the terrain, equipping yourself with mitigation strategies, being proactive, and staying vigilant for potential disruptions would guide you safely through.

Chapter 10. Resilience, Protection, and Troubleshooting: Effective Solutions

Behind each success story of digital communications and platforms lies a sturdy and robust system that guarantees secure and efficient operations. In the case of the Amazon Web Service (AWS), the backbone of this success is the AWS Certificate Manager (ACM). ACM's complex underpinning technologies, when used optimally, can create a fortress of security around your digital assets. Navigating the challenges and potential issues of ACM, though, demands a systematic understanding of resilient action plans and an knack for investigating and solving problems effectively.

10.1. Understanding ACM's Structure and Functionality

Firstly, a comprehensive grasp of ACM is critical. Fundamental to this understanding is the knowledge that ACM is a tool used to manage Secure Socket Layer/Transport Layer Security (SSL/TLS) certificates for your AWS services. It simplifies and automates certificate management tasks such as renewal and deployment, providing the digital certificates needed to enable HTTPS (SSL/TLS) for websites and applications.

10.2. Identifying Potential ACM issues

While ACM offers many benefits, its usage is not without potential challenges. The common problems include being unable to request a certificate as a result of the domain validation failing, certificates not appearing in ACM console despite a successful request, the SSL/TLS certificate not showing up in the AWS Management console, and getting a "domain not allowed" error when attempting to manage certificates.

These issues could be caused by a myriad of reasons ranging from DNS (Domain Name System) configuration issues, permissions and policy-setting issues, to common errors stemming from not being within the service limit.

10.3. Resilience Against ACM Problems

Problems are inevitable, but a resilient ACM setup can mitigate their impact significantly. The resiliency of your ACM setup greatly depends on your ability to troubleshoot, analyze, identify, and address the root cause of issues.

One important measure to undertake is regular and systematic checks of the DNS configuration. Ensuring your DNS configurations are properly set up enhances ACM's ability to conduct domain validation effectively. Closely monitoring domain registration details and its transferring process could also alert to any configuration irregularities.

Furthermore, an understanding of the IAM (Identity and Access Management) policies and permissions can preemptively ward off unnecessary issues related to access and use of your ACM. Regular audits of these permissions, coupled with a thorough understanding of principals, IAM policies, and resource-based permissions, are beneficial practices.

10.4. Protecting Your ACM Assets

As mentioned earlier, certificates play a critical protective role. The AWS Certificate Manager Private Certificate Authority (PCA) is a managed private CA service that helps you easily and securely manage the lifecycle of your private certificates. However, it could be expensive, and managing the budget might pose a challenge. One strategy could be to leverage the ACM PCA's ability to share resources in order to cut costs.

10.5. Troubleshooting ACM Issues

Knowing common problems can help troubleshoot effectively. However, the key to resolving any issue lies in an understanding of root causes.

If your domain validation is failing when you try requesting a certificate, it could be due to mismatched or incorrect DNS configuration or expired validation emails. It's crucial that the records in your DNS configuration match exactly with the record provided in the console. Also, ACM validation emails expire within 72 hours, so it's important to ensure they are checked and validated promptly.

In cases where the ACM certificate does not appear in the console, the issue may stem from regional discrepancies. Certificates are regional resources, and hence can be seen and managed only in the region in which they are created. Therefore, identifying and switching to the correct region can help solve this problem.

It's worth noting that the ability to troubleshoot effectively often hinges on a thorough understanding of ACM's inner workings. That's why it's so important to gain a familiarity with the AWS X.509 structure, constraints, and lifecycles.

In conclusion, ACM can be a powerful component of any AWS setup if managed and used effectively. Its benefits, from automation of certificate tasks to ensuring security in digital communications, far outweigh the potential challenges it presents. A thorough knowledge of how ACM works, a practical understanding of how to address potential issues, and a proactive approach in preventive measures can make mastering ACM an achievable task. Remember, resilience isn't just about bouncing back from difficulties but also bouncing forward, stronger and wiser.

Chapter 11. The Future Outlook and Ongoing Challenges with AWS Certificate Manager

As technology continues to evolve at breakneck speeds, so too does the landscape of cloud services, and particularly those offered by Amazon Web Services (AWS), including the Certificate Manager. In our forward-looking analysis of this service, there are specific key trends and challenges that we can identify.

11.1. Increased Use of Automation

One noticeable trend is the increasing reliance on automation. The automation of tasks decreases human errors and improves efficiency. The AWS Certificate Manager is no exception. Users can automate the process of deploying, renewing, and managing certificates, thereby saving time and increasing operational efficiency.

However, this shift towards automation isn't without challenges. Configuration errors can result in service disruptions, leading to operational and financial losses. Regular auditing of automation processes and use of tools that highlight configuration changes can help minimize potential disruptions.

11.2. Growing Cybersecurity Threats

Cybersecurity threats are ever-changing, with attackers continually finding new ways to exploit vulnerabilities. Encryption technologies, including digital certificates, are a prime area of focus.

The AWS Certificate Manager provides robust encryption capabilities, thereby ensuring data in transit remains secure. Unfortunately, as encryption becomes more complex, so do the threats. Therefore, it's important that users stay informed about the latest cybersecurity threats and apply appropriate defense strategies.

Enhanced security measures, such as the use of multifactor authentication and limiting permissions, should always be encouraged. Additionally, organizations should consider leveraging AWS CloudTrail, which logs account activity for security analysis, resource change tracking, and compliance auditing.

11.3. Cloud Interoperability

Cloud interoperability continues to be a challenge as different cloud service providers use different platforms and standards. Some organizations use multiple cloud services, resulting in complexity when managing digital certificates across platforms.

Using AWS Certificate Manager solely could be restrictive, as it's compatible only with specific AWS services. Going forward, AWS may need to consider improving the interoperability between its Certificate Manager and other cloud services.

11.4. The Rising Importance of Certificate Transparency

Certificate Transparency (CT) is a security mechanism that publicly logs every issued SSL/TLS certificate. It allows anyone to audit and monitor certificates, helping to spot misissuance and certificate abuse.

Although AWS Certificate Manager supports CT logging for its public SSL/TLS certificates, it doesn't offer CT log monitoring tools. Given the increasing importance of CT, AWS might have to consider providing built-in CT log monitoring tools to help users proactively detect potential misissuance.

11.5. Need for Locality-specific Compliance

Organizations that operate in multiple regions have to comply with country-specific or region-specific cybersecurity regulations. AWS provides a variety of services and tools to ensure compliance, including AWS Certificate Manager.

However, locality-specific compliance regulations are continually evolving, and becoming more challenging. Adherence to these regulations will demand constant updates and improvements in the Certificate Manager's features and capabilities.

In conclusion, the future looks promising for the AWS Certificate Manager, with automation and cybersecurity taking center stage. However, evolving cybersecurity threats, cloud interoperability issues, the importance of certificate transparency, and locality-specific regulatory compliance present significant challenges. AWS will need to continually innovate and adapt its Certificate Manager to remain relevant and effective in this changing landscape.